CONCEPTS AND INQUIRY:
The Educational Research Council
Social Science Program

AMERICAN COMMUNITIES

An Historical Community

WILLIAMSBURG, VIRGINIA

Prepared by the Social Science Staff
of the Educational Research Council of America

ALLYN AND BACON, INC.

BOSTON • ROCKLEIGH, N.J. • ATLANTA • DALLAS • BELMONT, CALIF.

This book was prepared by the following members of the Social Science Staff of the Educational Research Council:

Marie M. Richards, *Coordinator*

Ethel K. Howard, Helen Lin, Olga Meyer, Agnes M. Michnay, Mary Payne, *Assistants*

Mary Catherine McCarthy, *Editor-in-Chief*

Raymond English, *Director*

The Educational Research Council of America acknowledges the contributions of the Kettering Family Fund and the Martha Holden Jennings Foundation, which have made possible the Social Science Program of the Educational Research Council of America.

CONTENTS

MAPS

ACKNOWLEDGMENTS

PHOTOGRAPHS: J.C. ALLEN & SON, pp. 8-9 bottom. ALPHA PHOTO ASSOCIATES, p. 4 Adeije Hurley. BOWDOIN COLLEGE MUSEUM OF ART, BRUNSWICK, MAINE, p. 95. COLONIAL WILLIAMSBURG, pp. 47; 54 top-bottom; 58; 59; 63; 67; 68; 69; 76; 78; 82 right; 83; 84 right; 85; 89 right; 91. DPI, pp. 5; 13 top, Dick Davis; 13 bottom, George Roos; 34 bottom, G. Burkhardt; 42. EDITORIAL PHOTOCOLOR ARCHIVES, p. iv top left. FORD MOTOR COMPANY, p. 11. GRANT HEILMAN, p. iv right. INDEPENDENCE NATIONAL HISTORICAL PARK, PHILADELPHIA, p. 94 top left. INTERNATIONAL HARVESTER, p. iv bottom left. HAROLD M. LAMBERT, pp. 12-13 bottom. LIBRARY OF CONGRESS, pp. 28-9; 41; 50; 52. I. AND B. MC MILLAN, pp. 21; 64 bottom; 71 right; 72 right; 81 all; 82 left. R. NEIL RHODES, p. 1 right. PHOTO RESEARCHERS, pp. 8 left, Van Bucher; 8-9 top, Van Bucher; 9 top, Van Bucher; 34 top, Charles R. Belinky; 35, Van Bucher. *Pictorial Story of Jamestown* by J. Paul Hudson, pp. 25; 39. THOMAS JEFFERSON MEMORIAL FOUNDATION, p. 94 bottom. UNION PACIFIC RAILROAD, p. 12 left. RAPHO GUILLUMETTE, p. 9 bottom, Bruce Roberts. U.S. ARMY PHOTO, 1 top left. YALE UNIVERSITY ART GALLERY, pp. 120-1.

All photos not otherwise credited are the work of the Allyn and Bacon staff photographers.

ILLUSTRATIONS: MATT DELFINO, pp. 96; 98-9; 100-1; 102; 103; 104; 106-7; 108; 110; 112; 114-5; 116; 118; 119; 122. JOHN GRETZER, pp. 24; 27; 36; 38; 40; 48-9. MARIE MICHAL, pp. 14; 15; 16-7; 18. BILL MORRISON, p. 56.

Map design and compilation by Allyn and Bacon

A NOTE TO BOYS AND GIRLS

This book will help you find things out
for yourself.   It will help you to use
the things you know.

Think about the problems and the questions
as you read. They are marked ▶, ●, or ★.

This is what the marks mean:

- ▶   easy to solve,
- ●   harder to solve —
  more thinking is needed,
- ★   something extra —
  maybe for homework.

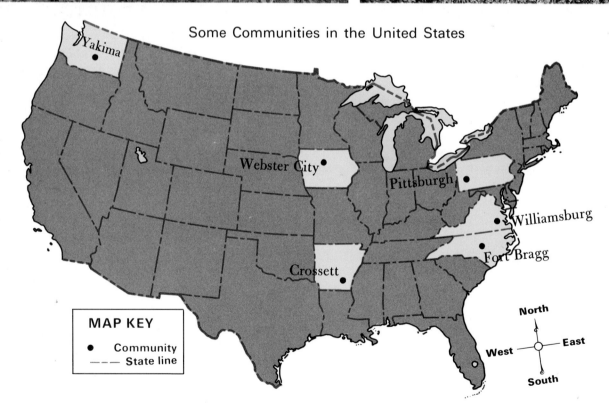

Some Communities in the United States

Yakima

Webster City

Pittsburgh

Williamsburg

Fort Bragg

Crossett

MAP KEY
● Community
- - - State line

North

West   East

South

Part One

Looking
Ahead

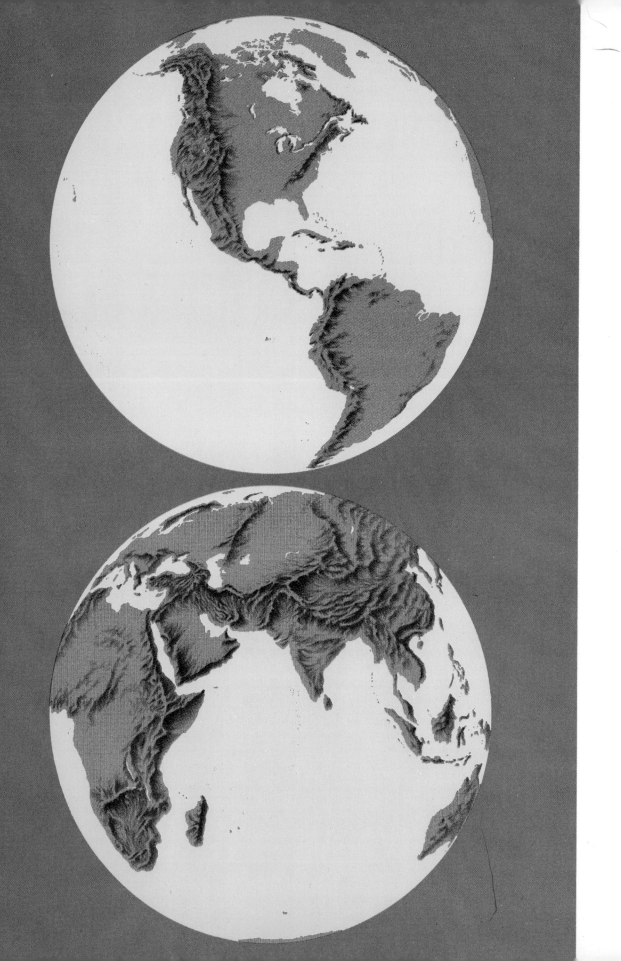

Learning About Communities in the United States

THE WORLD

The lands and waters of the Earth
Stretch north to south, and east to west.
The people of the world have lived
On lands and seas they liked the best.

● Name the seven continents and four oceans.
Find each on a globe.

▶ On which continent do you live?

People Live in Communities

Most people in the world live in communities.
These communities are changing all the time.
Sometimes communities change very slowly.

Sometimes they change rapidly. Some changes
are good. Some changes are not good.

- Has your community changed? How?
- Are some of the changes good?
- Are any of the changes *not* good?

Many of the Aborigines live in Central Australia.
Some Aborigines still live as they did thousands
of years ago. They go walkabout to look for food.
They do not wear many clothes. They do not live
in houses.

- How do Aborigines go walkabout?
- Why don't some Aborigines wear many clothes?
- What do they use for shelter?

Australian Aborigines spearing fish

Eskimos and dog teams on the tundra

The Eskimos in Barrow, Alaska learned to live
in a cold, cold land.   Then other people came to Barrow.
They brought with them new tools, new foods,
and new ways of living.   The Eskimos wanted
these new things.   They had to learn new skills
and make many changes.   Today the Barrow Eskimos
are changing rapidly.

We have studied three communities.
In some ways they are alike.   In some ways
they are different from one another.

- Tell how they are different.
- Tell how they are alike.

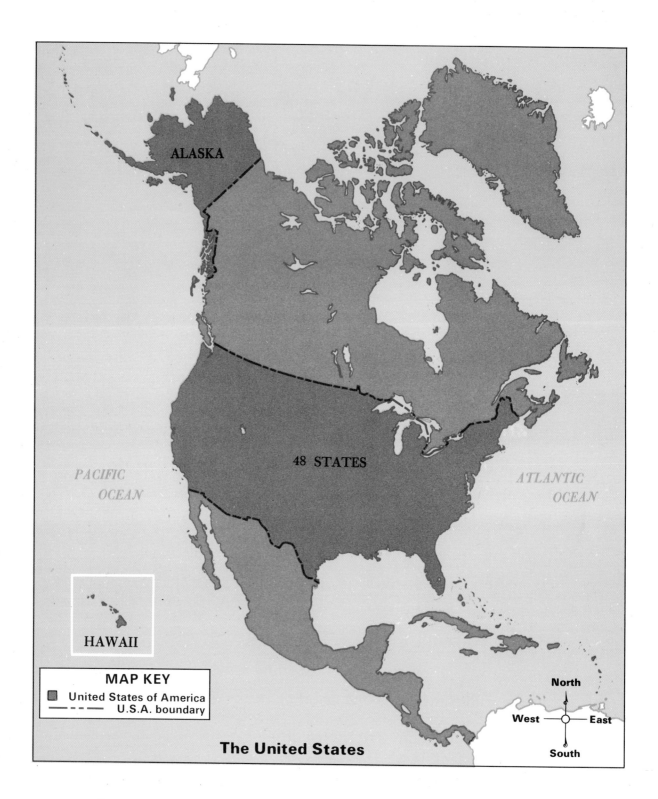

ALASKA

48 STATES

PACIFIC
OCEAN

ATLANTIC
OCEAN

HAWAII

MAP KEY

■ United States of America
— - — - — U.S.A. boundary

The United States

North

West ⊕ East

South

6

Our country is big.   It has 50 states.

Each state has many, many communities.

Some communities are BIG.

Some communities are MIDDLE SIZED.

Some communities are little.

OUR COUNTRY

Proudly

Words and Music by Olga Meyer

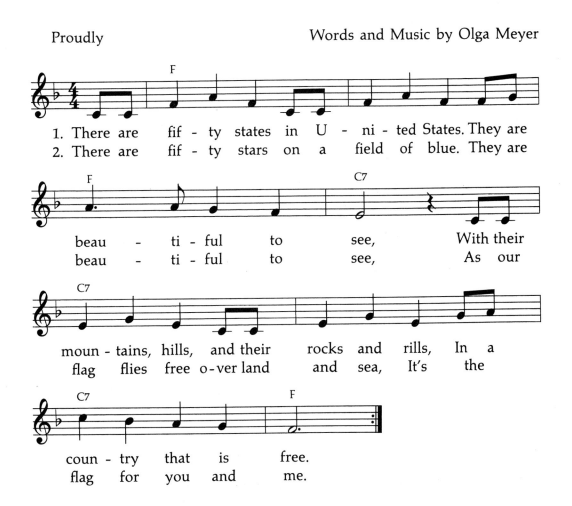

1. There are fif - ty states in U - ni - ted States. They are
2. There are fif - ty stars on a field of blue. They are

beau - ti - ful to see, With their
beau - ti - ful to see, As our

moun - tains, hills, and their rocks and rills, In a
flag flies free o-ver land and sea, It's the

coun - try that is free.
flag for you and me.

Areas in a Community

The parts of a community are called areas. There are different areas in a community. The areas are residential, commercial, industrial, recreational, and rural.

▶ Which area has many houses and some schools and churches?

▶ Which area has big factories?

▶ Which area has stores, offices, and banks?

▶ In which area are parks and zoos?

▶ Which area has fields and woods and few houses or stores?

Commercial

Rural (farm)

Residential

8

HOW DOES EACH AREA HELP THE OTHER AREAS?

Communities May Specialize

People in different areas of a community
depend on one another. People in one community
depend on people in other communities, too.
People in one community may make or grow
special things. They do **specialized** work.

Some people **specialize** in growing apples.
Some people specialize in growing corn.
Some communities specialize in making paper or steel.
Some communities provide a special service.

Industrial

Recreational

9

- People in one community specialize
  in growing corn. How do they depend
  on a community that specializes in making steel?

Mr. and Mrs. Green and their son, Jimmy,
live on a farm in Minnesota. Mr. Green has
a special kind of farm. It is a turkey farm.
Many people in many communities in the 50 states
depend on Mr. Green for their turkeys
for Thanksgiving Day dinners.

Jimmy has a new bicycle. It was made in a factory
in Little Rock, Arkansas. The factory makes
hundreds of bicycles every day. They are sent
to communities all over the United States.

Mrs. Green bought some oranges at the market.
They came all the way from Florida.
Oranges do not grow in Minnesota.

▶ How do you think Florida oranges came to be
  in a Minnesota store?

Mr. Green drives a car. It was put together
in Michigan. Before it was put together,
many special parts had to be sent
from many other communities to Michigan.

▶ How did a car made in Michigan
  get to Minnesota?

Men working in an automobile factory

Some people depend on Mr. Green for turkeys.
The Green family depends on many people
in other communities for things they need and want.
The Greens do not have to grow their own oranges
or make their own cars or bicycles. They can buy
these things because some communities
do special work.

- ▶ How did Mr. Green get the money for a bicycle?
- ● How does specializing help us have
  many goods and services?
- ● Why does specializing make communities
  depend on one another?

Transportation

Our country is big. But things can be sent
from one state to another. They can be sent
from a community on the West Coast to one
on the East Coast. Each community needs
some kind of transportation.

- Look at the pictures. Tell something
  about each kind of transportation.

Truck trailers are carried on railroad flatcars.
At the end of the trip they are taken
off the flatcars and hitched to trucks.

Freight train

Moving van

12

Jet freight plane

▶ Can you think of other kinds of transportation?

● Name some things people send from one place
to another.

▶ Why do they send these things?

▶ How do people and special things
get from one community to another?

● If we did not have good transportation,
communities could not do specialized work.
Why is this so?

Cargo boat

13

Communication

People in communities can also tell things
to one another.

This is a message.

This is Tom.   This is Jeff.

Tom is telling Jeff something.   Tom is communicating
with Jeff.   Jeff lives next door to Tom.
When one person tells something to another person,
they are **communicating.**

Tom lives in California.   Tom's grandmother
lives in New York.

▶ How can Tom communicate
   with his grandmother?

● Can you think of ways to communicate
   without talking?

14

Some ways of communicating

Communication and transportation bring people together. The people in one community can find out what people in other communities are doing. They can find out what people in other communities make or grow. They can buy things from other communities.

Communication and transportation make it possible for communities to do specialized work.

Communication and transportation help in other ways, too. They help people share ideas. They help people learn from one another. They help people have fun together. Most important, they help people understand one another.

We shall think about these things when we study some communities in the United States. We shall ask ourselves questions about these communities.

Questions About a Community

Do you remember these questions about a community?

1. Where is it?

2. What does it look like?

3. What kinds of weather does it have?

4. What kinds of people live there?

5. What kinds of houses do the people have?

6. What food do they eat?

7. What religions do
   the people have?

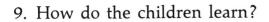

8. What work do they do?

9. How do the children learn?

10. How do the people have fun?

11. What rules and government
    does the community have?

12. Is the community changing?

Here are two more questions we will ask
about communities in the United States:

13. What kinds of transportation
and communication do they have?

14. Does the community grow
    or make something special?

These questions are social science questions.
Social science is the study of people in communities.
   Some of the answers to these questions
will be the same for each community we study.
Some will be different. The ways these communities
are different are very important. Learning about them
will help us understand how people live on the Earth.

20

Part Two

An
Historical
Community:
Williamsburg, Virginia

CHAPTER 1

Englishmen Come to a New Land

Crossing the Atlantic Ocean

Long, long ago three ships sailed across the Atlantic Ocean. Men from England were on those ships. They were on their way to the new land called America.

Sometimes storms made the waves very high. Many of the men became sick. Many were afraid. But they did not turn back.

One — two — three — four — five long months they sailed. Then one day in May they saw land. It was the land we now call Virginia.

The men sailed up a large river. They named it the James River for King James in England.

Boats like these were used by the English settlers who came to America in 1607.

Green grass covered the land on both sides of the river. Wildflowers grew in the grass. Trees were everywhere — trees that could be used for building houses.

Landing in the New World

When the men tried to come ashore, some Indians shot arrows at them. The Englishmen shot their guns. The Indians ran away.

Indians shot arrows at the Englishmen.

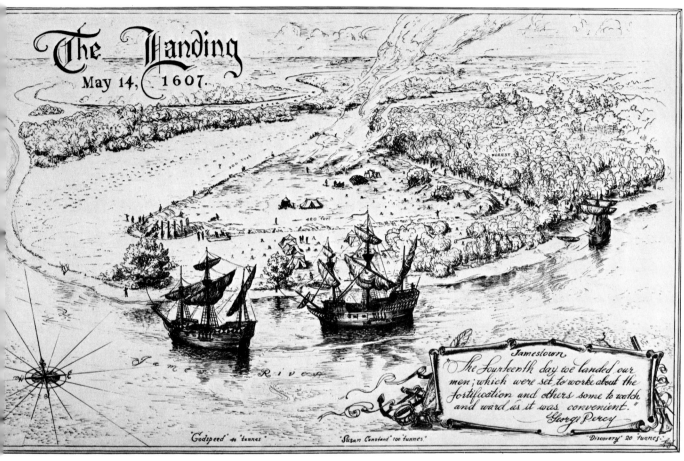

The peninsula in the James River

The men sailed on up the James River. They came
to a peninsula. Then they went ashore.

▶ What is a peninsula?

▶ Do you remember that Alaska is a peninsula?

● Why do you think the Indians shot arrows
  at the Englishmen?

25

The wall around the fort

The Fort at Jamestown

When the men went ashore, they looked around.
They liked what they saw. The land was flat.
They could sail their ships close to the shore.
The peninsula had water on three sides.
It would help protect them from Indians.

● How would the peninsula help protect the men
from the Indians?

There were animals in the forest and fish
in the river. There were many trees. The Englishmen
decided to stay, or **settle,** there.

They built a fort. Inside the fort they built
little houses. They built a little church and
a storehouse. This **settlement** was called Jamestown.

● How did the men use the animals and the trees?

26

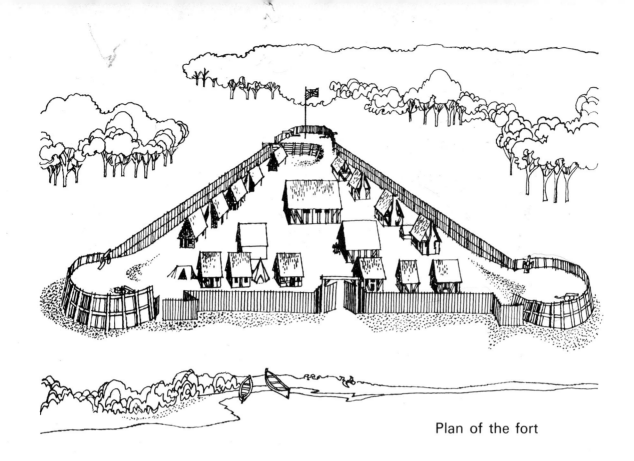

Plan of the fort

Inside the fort

Colonists from England

More men came to Jamestown from England. They brought food, clothing, and tools. They brought seeds for planting food crops. The settlement at Jamestown became the first English **colony** in America. The men were called **colonists.**

Soon women came from England, too. They came to marry the colonists and start homes in the new country.

As the years went by, more English families came to Virginia. New settlements were started.

Many families built their homes on the lowlands
beside the rivers.   One settlement was started
on higher land north of Jamestown.
It was named Williamsburg.

- Why were many homes built near the rivers?
▶ What country did the colonists
   come from?
▶ Where did the first English colonists
   live in America?

English women came
to Jamestown.

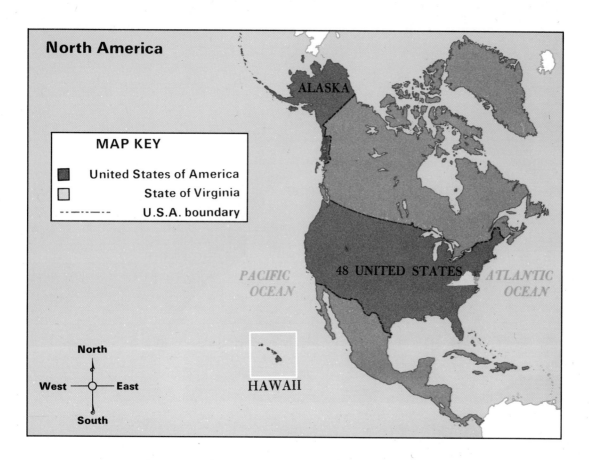

Finding Virginia

The James River and Jamestown are in Virginia. Where is Virginia?

First, it will help you to know on which continent Virginia is found.

Look at the map above.

▶ What is the name of the continent?

Look at the map key.

▶ Find the United States.
▶ What ocean is east of the United States?

▶ What ocean is west of the United States?

▶ Find the State of Virginia.

▶ Is Virginia in the eastern or western part
of the United States?

Virginia is part of the continent of North America.
Virginia is part of a country, too.

Look at the map below.

▶ What is the name of the country?

▶ Which of the 50 states are not shown?

▶ Find the State of Virginia.

● What direction is Virginia from your state?

▶ What ocean is east of Virginia?

Where is Virginia?

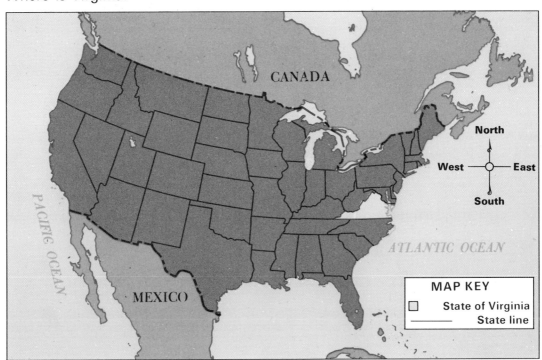

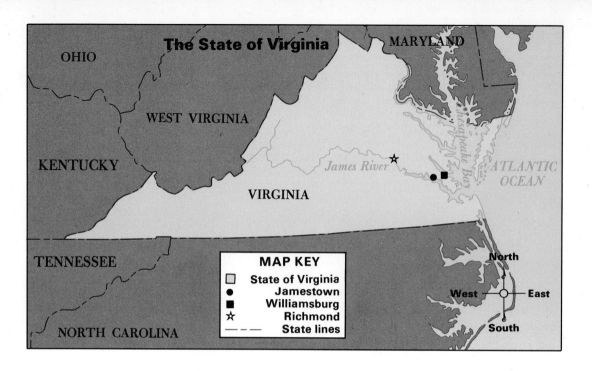

We have seen Virginia on a map of North America.
It looked very small. We have seen Virginia on a map
of the United States. It looked a little larger.
Now let us look at a state map of Virginia.
A state map will give us a better look at Virginia.

● What does the map show you?

Physical Features

The James River starts in the mountains of Virginia.
It flows down, down, down to the ocean. As it gets
nearer the ocean, it gets wider. It flows slower
and slower. Then it flows into the ocean.

▶ In what direction does the James River flow?
▶ Into what ocean does the James River flow?

A part of Virginia touches the Atlantic Ocean
and Chesapeake Bay. It is called the **coastline.**
The land near the coast is low.

> ▶ Trace the Virginia coastline with your finger.
> ▶ Is Jamestown north or south
>   of the James River?

The land near the James River is low. It is sandy.
There are swamps near the ocean and river.
Swamps are places where the land is wet and mushy.
Mosquitoes and other insects live in swamps.
Swamps are not healthy places for settlements.
Many men in Jamestown became sick and died
during the first year.

Williamsburg was built on higher land
north of Jamestown.

> ▶ Find Williamsburg.

Swamps near the James River

Away from the river and ocean, the land is higher.
There are rolling hills. Farther west in Virginia
there are high mountains. The mountains are beautiful.
They are covered with evergreen trees.

34

Virginia's Climate

It is not too hot in Virginia. It is not too cold.
The summers are warm, with some hot days.
The winters are cool.
There is enough rain for growing food.
There is enough rain to grow fine grasses and trees.
Very little snow falls near the ocean.
There is more snow on the hills and in the mountains.

CHAPTER 2

The Indians of Virginia

The First Americans

The first Americans were Indians.
They were the aborigines of America.
Some people said the Indians had red skin.
Their skin was not really red. It was more like brown
or copper — the color of an old penny. They had
black hair. Sometimes they put paint on their bodies —
red, white, or black. Indians liked bright colors.

The forests were full of deer and other wild animals.
Indian men hunted the animals for food.
They fished in the waters. The Indians made
all their own hunting and fishing tools.

Indian women planted the food **crops.**
They raised corn, beans, squash, pumpkins,
and potatoes. It was hard work.

Indians burned and dug out the insides of logs
to make canoes.

The women also made the clothing. They used the skins of animals. In summer, the Indian men and children wore few clothes.

▶ What other aborigines have you read about?

There were many tribes of Indians. Each tribe had different ways. Often the tribes would fight each other. The Indians lived in villages. They built fences around their villages. Then they could protect themselves from other Indian tribes.

In Virginia, the Indians lived in round houses. Little trees were used to make a **frame.** Bark was taken from the trees. It was put over the frame.

Indian houses in Virginia

Indians trading with Englishmen

Indians and Englishmen

The Indians watched the Englishmen
after the landing at Jamestown. The Indians got used
to seeing the Englishmen. They became friendly.
They even traded. They traded corn and deer meat
for beads, tools, and knives.

Englishmen hunting in the forest

The Indians saw the Englishmen chop down trees.
Englishmen used iron axes. They could chop down
the biggest trees. How the Indians wished
they had such a tool!

▶   Why would an Indian want to trade corn
    for an axe or a knife?
●   Would the Indians trade corn for guns?
    Tell why or why not.

40

The Englishmen cut down more and more trees.
They built houses and forts with the wood.
They hunted the deer in the forests for food.
The Indians did not like this. They had hunted
in these forests for a long time. The Indians
killed some of the Englishmen.

Often the Englishmen were hungry.
Some became sick and died. A few men were brave
and helped the rest. Some asked the Indians
for food. The Indians gave them food.
For a time, there was peace between Englishmen
and Indians.

- How did the Indians feel
  about the Englishmen? Why?

Early settlers building homes

CHAPTER 3

Colonists in Virginia

Tobacco — As Good as Money

Some of the colonists thought they would find gold.
They did not find gold. Gold is not part
of Virginia's natural environment. The colonists began
to learn more about their natural environment. They found
that the land and the climate were just right
for growing **tobacco.** And people in England
wanted to buy tobacco.

Some families had big fields of tobacco.
They wanted bigger and bigger fields.
The more tobacco the colonists grew, the more they
could send to England. The more they sent to England,
the more things they could get from England.
Tobacco was as good as money.

43

Tobacco fields in Virginia

Before long, most of the flat land and rolling hills
were used for growing tobacco. The Indians
were pushed back — back into the forests.
They did not like this.

- Why did the Indians not like
  being pushed back into the forests?

The men who owned the big fields of tobacco
could not do all the work themselves.   They did not want
to do it, either.   Working in the fields was hard work.
The tobacco fields were very big, and everything
had to be done by hand.   Many owners wanted Indians
to do the work.   But the Indians would not.

Tobacco was shipped from docks in Virginia.

45

Bond servants working in tobacco fields

Colonists wanted more workers to come
from England. Many English people wanted
to come to America. But they did not have
enough money to pay for the trip. Rich colonists
agreed to pay for the trip. In return, these people
agreed to work for the colonists for five or six
or more years. They were called **bond servants.**

Bond servants were not paid with money.
Their masters gave them food, clothing, and shelter.
When their years of work were over, they were free.

Most bond servants worked in the fields.
Still, there were not enough workers. The fields
were so big that more and more workers were needed.

▶ Why was tobacco as good as money?

▶ Why did people want bigger tobacco fields?

- ▶ Who worked in the tobacco fields?
- ▶ Why were more workers needed?
- ● What do you think bond servants did when they were free?

Black People Come to Virginia

One day a ship came up the river to Jamestown. It was not an English ship.

"Where is that ship from?" asked one of the men who was watching.

"It is a Dutch ship. I can tell by the flag," said another man. "Let us see who is on the ship."

The first black people arrive at Jamestown.

Some of the people went to the ship.   They
were surprised by what they saw.   Twenty black people
had been taken off the ship.   They were standing
in a group.   They looked unhappy and afraid.
They had been taken away from their homes in Africa.

A man from the boat said, "We need food
for the people on our boat.   You need workers
in the tobacco fields.   We will trade these black people
for food."

The colonists traded food for the black men.
The black people were put to work in the fields
with the bond servants.   At first, they were treated
like bond servants.   They were set free after five,
six, or more years.

As time went on, more black people were taken
from their homes in Africa.   Many were brought
to Virginia.   There they were traded or sold.

48   A master looks on as his slaves put tobacco
in barrels. Then the slaves roll the barrels
down to the ships at the docks.

Owners of big tobacco fields did not want to lose
all their workers after five years.
They freed white bond servants.
But they forced black people to become slaves.

A **slave** was not free to do as he wished.
He belonged to the person who bought him.
This person was called a master. A slave
had to work for his master for the rest
of his life. The master provided food, clothes,
and shelter. Slaves were not allowed
to own anything.

● Think. How would you feel if you were:

    taken from your home?

    taken to a strange country?

    not able to understand the language

      of the country?

    sold to a strange man?

    made to do hard work without pay?

    made to do whatever your master ordered?

Slaves were forced to work so hard that
some of the colonists became very rich. They got
more and more land. They bought more slaves
to work on the land. These colonists
became important people in Virginia.
They were able to get fine things from England.

Rich colonists wore fine clothes from England.

They got clothes, furniture, and dishes. But
the slaves did not have those fine things.
They could not own anything.

▶   Why didn't the poor people have slaves?

Virginia Men Help Make Laws

When people live together, they need rules.
Rules make living together safer and easier.

▶   Tell about a rule you have at home.
▶   Tell about a rule at school.
●   What would happen if there were no rules?

Rules are sometimes called **laws.**
The Virginia colonists needed laws. People
in Jamestown needed laws. Other settlements in Virginia
needed laws, too. What rules and government
did these settlements have?

For about ten years, the laws for the people
of Virginia were made by men in England. That was
because Virginia belonged to England. Jamestown
was made the capital of Virginia. A **Governor**
was sent to Jamestown from England. It was
the Governor's job to see that the laws of England
were obeyed in Virginia.

Men of Virginia met with the Governor to help make laws for Virginia.

The men of Virginia were Englishmen. They believed that they should have the right to help make laws for their communities. The government of England agreed. The Virginia colonists were happy to hear the good news. Now they could help make the laws for their own communities.

The people in Virginia chose certain men.
These men would speak for the people of Virginia.
The men met with the Governor in Jamestown.
Each man spoke about problems in his part of Virginia.
Then they all helped to make laws for Virginia.

The men went back to their own settlements.
They told the colonists about the talks
with the Governor.   They told how they helped
to make Virginia's laws.   Virginia colonists
felt proud and free.

▶ Why did Virginia men think of themselves
as Englishmen?

● Why did they feel proud and free?

● Do you think slaves were allowed
to help make laws? Why or why not?

CHAPTER 4

A New Town in Virginia: Williamsburg

The Capital Moves to Williamsburg

Jamestown was an important town for a long time.
But the land was swampy. Many people died
from disease.

There had been fires, too. Twice all the buildings
burned. The second time, the lawmakers said,
"Let us move the capital to higher land away
from the swamps. The College of William and Mary
is to the north. Let us build a town there."

- What is a college?

A fine palace was built for the Governor.
A beautiful building was built where the lawmakers
could meet. It was called the **Capitol.**

- Where is the Capitol of the United States?
  Who works there?

55

The College of William and Mary in George Washington's time
and as it looks now

The town was named Williamsburg. It was named after King William, the new King of England.

Now Williamsburg became an important town. Lawmakers from all parts of Virginia came to the Capitol. They met and talked about many things. Mostly, they talked about the English colonies in America.

Look at the map of Virginia on page 32.

▶ Find Jamestown and Williamsburg.

Williamsburg's Main Street

The main street of Williamsburg was called Duke of Gloucester (GLAHS ter) Street. The Capitol was at one end of the street. The College of William and Mary was at the other end.

This is a drawing of the main street in Williamsburg.

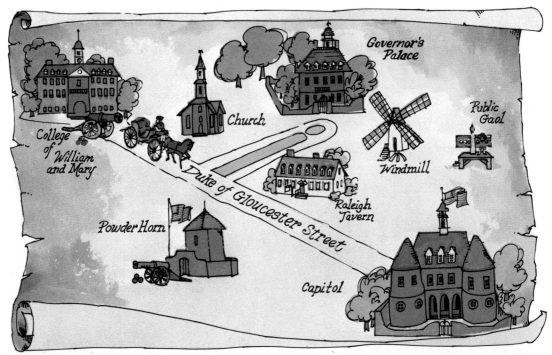

This street also had beautiful homes and gardens.
Many rich people lived in Williamsburg.
The Governor had parties in the palace. The parties
were all very grand. The men wore white wigs.
They wore silver buckles on their shoes.
The ladies wore long dresses with wide, wide skirts.
The dresses were made of silk and satin.

The Idea of Independence

Williamsburg was an important town for many years.
That was a long, long time ago. Why do we
want to know about Williamsburg now? It is
because a very important idea began in Williamsburg.
That important idea was the idea of **independence.**

All the lands where the English people lived
in America were called **colonies.** The colonies
belonged to England. For a long time the colonies
got along well with England. People in America
lived much as people did in England.

Then trouble grew between the colonies
and England. Colonists did not agree with many rules
made by the King's government. The King's government
said, "You must send the things you grow or make
to England. You may not send these things
to any other country. You must buy only the things we sell.

And you must use only English ships."
The colonists did not like this kind of rule.

● Why didn't the colonists like the King's orders?

The King's government needed money.
The colonists had to pay more taxes. The colonists
did not like this. All over the American colonies
men were meeting in groups. They talked about taxes.
They talked about the King's government.

"Why should lawmakers back in England
tell us what to do?" they asked. "We should make
the laws about our taxes."

▶ Why did the men meet in the colonies?

A room in the Raleigh Tavern. Virginia men met here to talk things over.

Patrick Henry

More and more things made the colonists unhappy.
More meetings were held. The colonists wanted to do
something about their problems. The people of Virginia
led the way. Men of Virginia met in Williamsburg.
Often, they met at the Raleigh (RAH lee) Tavern.
George Washington and Thomas Jefferson came there.
A young man named Patrick Henry came there, too.

Patrick Henry was a lawmaker. He was
a good speaker, too. Men liked to hear him speak.
Many were ready to do what he said. Patrick Henry
spoke out against the King's government.

"We are free men," he said. "We should have
the same liberty as if we were living in England.
If we have nothing to say about our government,
then we have lost our freedom."

Patrick Henry said that the King's government was taking the colonists' freedom away. He and other colonists began to think of disobeying the King's laws. Patrick Henry's ideas were printed in newspapers. People in all the colonies read them. They read what other Virginia lawmakers said, too. Colonists began to think of themselves as Americans instead of Englishmen.

Many said, "Let us fight for our rights. There are many of us in America now. We can have our own country. Then we can be independent. We can make our own laws. We can choose what is best for our country."

The colonists' ideas about independence began in Williamsburg. Ideas about starting a new country — our country — came from Williamsburg.

Inside the printing office in Williamsburg. Patrick Henry's words were printed here.

60

- How did Virginia colonists
  lead the way in ideas about independence?

Ideas and words about independence were
only the beginning. Later, the colonies went to war
with England. George Washington was the General
of the American Army. The colonies won the war.
They started a new country. It was called
the **United States.** It was free from England.

The head of the United States government
is a **President** — not a king. George Washington
and Thomas Jefferson both became Presidents.

- What Virginia men were important
  in the government of the United States? Why?

The Capital Is Moved Away from Williamsburg

More and more people came from many countries
in Europe. They wanted to live in a country
that was free. The people began to move west.
Virginia wanted to move its capital farther west.
It was moved to Richmond.

Look at the map of Virginia on page 32.

▶ Find Richmond. It is the capital
of Virginia today.

When the capital was moved from Jamestown
to Williamsburg, Jamestown stopped growing.
Many people moved to other towns.
Other towns were busier. There were more jobs.
The same thing happened to Williamsburg when
the capital was moved to Richmond. Lawmakers
no longer met at the Capitol in Williamsburg.
It was no longer a busy center. Soon it was just
a little country town. The buildings were not
cared for. The windows of the old Raleigh Tavern
were broken. Its walls were not painted.
Then it burned down and was not rebuilt.
Many beautiful trees were cut down.
The pretty gardens were gone.

Duke of Gloucester Street after the capital was moved to Richmond

When new buildings were put up,
many old houses and shops were torn down.
New buildings and old buildings were crowded
together. The town began to look shabby.
It seemed that old Williamsburg would just
fade away and be forgotten.

CHAPTER 5

Restored Williamsburg

The Great Idea

About forty years ago, some people
in Williamsburg had a great idea. They wanted
to restore Williamsburg. **Restore** means
to fix up. They wanted Williamsburg to look
just as it did when it was first built.

Long ago, great Americans had lived
in Williamsburg. They had met and talked
at the Raleigh Tavern. They had made laws
for Virginia in the Capitol. They had visited
the palace to see the Governor. They had walked
on Duke of Gloucester Street under tall trees.
Many had worshipped at the old church.

Ideas about independence for the colonies
began in Williamsburg. They spread
to all the colonies. Because of these ideas,
the colonies went to war with England.

Two pictures of Duke of Gloucester Street today

They won the war and started a new country.
Williamsburg was an important town.

- ▶ Which great Americans lived
  in Williamsburg long ago?
- ● What were some ideas that began
  in Williamsburg?
- ▶ What new country was started
  by the American colonies?

There was hardly anything left of the old town
of Williamsburg. It was almost forgotten.
People who cared thought it was a shame.
A place where great Americans had lived
should be saved. The old buildings should be
rebuilt. The streets and gardens of the town
should be restored. The shops and stores
should be fixed up. Then Americans could see
the place where so many important ideas began.
They could see where great Americans lived.
Americans should remember such places.

- ● Why would Americans today
  want to visit restored Williamsburg?

Many workers would be needed to restore
Williamsburg. It would cost a lot of money.
Dr. W. Goodwin was a minister in Williamsburg.

Dr. W. Goodwin and Mr. Rockefeller

His church had been restored. He knew
that John D. Rockefeller, Jr. was a rich man.
He thought Mr. Rockefeller would be interested
in restoring Williamsburg.

Dr. Goodwin talked to Mr. Rockefeller
about the idea. He said, "In this way,
the future may learn from the past."
Mr. Rockefeller agreed to help. He gave
the money needed for restoring Williamsburg.

The Work of Restoring

Plans for restoring Williamsburg began
at once. It took a year to finish the plans.
There was so much work to be done!

First, people had to find out just how
the town looked long ago.   They went to libraries
in England, France, Canada, and the United States.
They read old books and letters.   They looked
at old pictures and maps.   The College of William
and Mary had an old map.   It was made
by a soldier in George Washington's army.
It showed where most of the old buildings stood.

▶   Why did people look at old pictures and maps?

Next, hundreds of modern buildings
had to be moved out of the area.   Then the area
to be restored was cleaned up.   Lines were drawn
to mark the places where old buildings stood.
Streets and paths were also marked.

Workers restoring buildings

Then the workers started to dig. They found
parts of old buildings. They found basements,
steps, and walks. They found other things, too.

- What other things might the diggers have found?

At last, the building and fixing up began.
The Governor's Palace, the Raleigh Tavern,
and the Capitol were rebuilt. They look
just as they did long ago. The furniture
inside each building is antique (an TEEK).
Antique means very old.

Many old houses were rebuilt. Flowers
and trees were planted. Gardens were restored.
Little shops were built. People who visit
Williamsburg can see how boots, wigs, cloth,
bread, and other things were made long ago.

Inside the Raleigh Tavern

Duke of Gloucester Street is once more lined
with tall trees. Visitors can now walk
where great Americans walked long ago. They can see
where our idea of government had its beginning.

- Tell some of the things that had to be done
  to restore Williamsburg.
- Why did people plan to restore the town?
- ▶ How did Mr. Rockefeller help?
- Why do you think people visit Williamsburg?

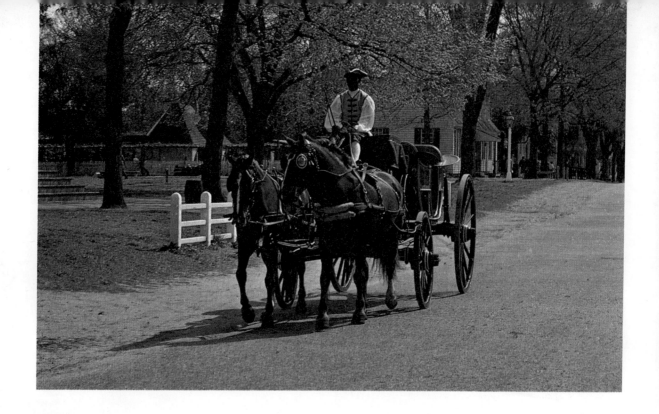

Duke of Gloucester Street

Let us visit restored Williamsburg.
Look at the picture of Duke of Gloucester Street.
There are no cars. We feel that this street belongs
to a long-ago time. George Washington walked
on this street. People who lived a long time ago
had a different way of life.

Beautiful trees are on both sides of the street.
The houses look as they did 200 years ago.
Goods are carried in carts with two wheels.
They are pulled by oxen.

> ▶ What other kinds of transportation
> were used in old Williamsburg?

Mr. and Mrs. Leeds work as guides
in restored Williamsburg. They dress the way
people in Williamsburg dressed many years ago.
This helps people feel they are really visiting
an old, old town. Mr. and Mrs. Leeds will tell us
about different places in old Williamsburg.

- Why do you think guides are needed
  in Williamsburg?

The Governor's Palace

"Come with me," says Mr. Leeds.
"I will show you a beautiful building.
It is just like the palace that used to be
in Williamsburg. Seven English Governors lived
in the palace. Later, two Virginia Governors,
Patrick Henry and Thomas Jefferson, lived there."

The furniture inside the palace is antique.
Every room is big and beautiful. The dishes,
the silver, and even the wallpaper are as they were
years ago. There is so much to see.

Front of the Governor's Palace

Back of the Governor's Palace

The ballroom

"This big, big room is the ballroom," says Mr. Leeds.
"This is where the Governor had parties for his guests.
Men in wigs and ladies with beautiful dresses
danced in this ballroom. They danced a slow dance
called the **minuet.** They also did a faster dance
called the **Virginia Reel.**"

The gardens outside the palace are beautiful.
They are gay with flowers and hedges.

Gardens of the Governor's Palace

The Capitol

Mr. Leeds asks, "Do you see that building
at the end of Duke of Gloucester Street?"

"Oh," you say, "I saw a picture of that building
in a book.   It is the Capitol of old Williamsburg."

The Capitol Building

The furniture and toys are antiques. It is fun
to see what children had many years ago.

Do you know what colonial children did for fun?
They liked to roll a hoop with a stick. Walking
on stilts was fun, too. Boys liked to play soldier.
And, of course, girls played with dolls.

Boys and girls played marbles and tag. They played
hopscotch and blindman's buff.

▶   Which of these games do you play?

The Public Gaol (Jail)

In old Williamsburg, jail was spelled "gaol."
Although these words look different, they sound
alike and mean the same thing.

When Williamsburg was the capital of Virginia,
the laws were very strict. Do you see
the brick building in the picture on page 78 ?
It was the **Public Gaol.** Inside are small,
dark rooms. People who broke the law
were locked in these rooms. They were kept there
until judges decided on their punishment.
One time, 13 pirates were locked up.

Very serious crimes were punished with death.
Less serious crimes were punished in other ways.

Locked in the pillory. The man to the right is locked in the stocks.

People were not usually kept in the gaol
for punishment. The gaol was too small for this.
There were not many guards. Sometimes the **pillory**
or the **stocks** were used. People could not get loose
from the pillory or the stocks. Everyone in the town
could come and look at them. People in the pillory
or the stocks felt very much ashamed.

Look at the picture of a pillory. The woman
has her hands and head in holes. She cannot get out.
She cannot sit down. Do you see the locks and chains?

- ▶ Make believe you are in a pillory. Stand that way for a time. How do you feel?
- ▶ How do you think a lawbreaker would feel if his friends saw him? What if someone who was *not* a friend saw him?

Sometimes lawbreakers were put in the stocks. The person who was in the stocks had to sit with his feet up for a long time.

- ▶ Try sitting like this for a while. How would you feel if you had to sit like this for a very long time?
- ▶ How would you feel if boys threw sticks or stones at you while you were locked in the pillory or stocks?

Tourists have fun here now. But it was not fun for the lawbreakers.

Fifes and Drums

Listen to the music! Here come men playing fifes and drums. **Fifes** look like little flutes and sound like whistles. The music makes you feel like marching.

Next, the men stand like soldiers and drill.

Fifers and Drummers

They fire old guns. How noisy the guns are! You
can see and smell the smoke of the black gunpowder.

Gunpowder and guns were kept in a brick building
called "The Powder Horn." A high brick wall
was built to protect this building.

Why was such a building needed? Every healthy man
had to learn how to be a soldier. He had to help
protect his town. The guns and powder had to be kept
in a safe place.

Today you may go into "The Powder Horn."
You may go in to see
the old guns. You may see
other things used by soldiers
long ago.

- Who protects American
  towns today?

80

"The Powder Horn"

Shopping
in Williamsburg

Little Shops

There is so much to see in Williamsburg.
We can not see everything in one day. The next morning
Mr. and Mrs. Leeds take us to see many little shops.
People in the shops make things as the people
of old Williamsburg did.

"You may buy things in these shops," says Mrs. Leeds.

When Williamsburg was the capital of Virginia,
most things were done by hand. Each shopkeeper
learned to do one thing well. In this way,
many different things could be made. Let us see
what some of these things were.

▶ Most things were made by hand long ago.
How are most things made in America today?

Wigmaker

We come to a shop window full of **wigs.** We see
big wigs, little wigs, colored wigs, and white wigs.
Long ago, a **wigmaker** made wigs for men and women.
Some Virginia men wore colored wigs for everyday.
For dress up, they wore white wigs. Why did men
wear wigs? It was the style, long ago.
Ladies wore wigs at fancy parties.

▶ Are wigs worn today? Who wears wigs?

▶ What are men's hair styles like today?

82

Weaver

Many years ago much of the clothing was made by hand. Most houses had a spinning wheel and a loom. The women would spin thread on the **spinning wheel.**

Every town had a weaver. The **weaver** would weave the thread into cloth on a **loom.** Then the cloth was made into clothes.

The rich people often got their cloth from England. Special workers made the clothes. These clothes were very fine. Only the rich people could buy the cloth because it cost so much.

- What changes have taken place since then?
- What has made the difference?
▶ How are most clothes made today?

Bootmaker

The **bootmaker** sits on a bench and makes shoes.
In Williamsburg long ago, the bootmaker was
a busy man. He made shoes for everyone.
The shoes had square toes. There was no right
or left shoe. Both were the same.

Today, the bootmaker has old tools on the wall. He
uses them to show tourists how the shoes were made.

▶ How are shoes made today?

▶ Where do you get your shoes?

● Do you have left and right shoes? Why?

84

Baker

Our noses tell us we are near a **bakery**.
The baker mixes the dough with his hands.
He shapes it into loaves.   Then he bakes it
in a brick oven.   Gingerbread and cookies
are cooling on the table.   Shall we buy some?

▶   How is bread made today?
●   How do you think the brick oven is heated?

Blacksmith

This shop has a sign shaped like a horse's head.
Clang! Clang! Clang! What is going on in this shop?
Mr. Leeds tells us it is a blacksmith's shop.
The blacksmith was a very busy man. The **blacksmith**
had to make all kinds of things out of iron.
He made horseshoes, wagon wheels, and nails.
He made candlesticks, tools, and kettles.

The pictures on these pages show us how
the blacksmiths worked. They heated the iron
in the fire to make it soft. Then they could bend
and shape it with a hammer. Do you see
the horseshoes above the fire?

- How is iron made today?
- What things are made of iron?

fire—to bend the iron

hammer—to shape the iron

at work making horseshoes

anvil—to hammer on

horseshoes—made from iron

Other Crafts

There are many other things to see. In one shop, we see a silversmith. A **silversmith** makes things out of silver. In another, a man is making guns.

► Are guns made by hand today?

● How are silver spoons and cups made today?

A silversmith at work

Guns were made by hand, too.

88

Soap and candles were made by hand. It looks like fun. It was not much fun for the colonists.

There are other small shops that have things to sell. Tourists can buy pictures, silver, and furniture. They can buy candles and dishes.

Making candles

Making soap

The Windmill

This **windmill** has big stones inside. When the wind
turns the sails of the mill, the big stones move.
They grind corn into fine **meal** for baking.
Tourists, and people who live in Williamsburg
may buy the meal.

- ▶ What do people do with cornmeal?
- ▶ What makes the mill work?
- ★ Find out how corn is ground today.

90

Living in Williamsburg

Living in Williamsburg today is almost like living in any other town. One thing makes it different. Many tourists come to see restored Williamsburg. So most of the people that live there provide goods and services for the tourists.

- What services are needed in restored Williamsburg? (Clue: What needs and wants do tourists have?)
- What goods are needed in restored Williamsburg?

The people who live in restored Williamsburg live as we do. They have electricity, but the wires are under the ground. They have TV sets, but the aerials are hidden. This helps to make the main street beautiful.

Other families live outside the restored area.

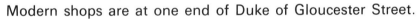

Modern shops are at one end of Duke of Gloucester Street.

School children and teachers on their way to visit old Williamsburg

Many Tourists

Every year many tourists visit Williamsburg.
They come from all over the world. They come
to see the places where great Americans worked.
When Americans see Williamsburg, they think of men
like Washington, Jefferson, and Patrick Henry.
They remember how hard these men worked
for freedom. Americans honor these men.

Many people who visit Williamsburg think
about freedom in this country today. They think
that we must work hard to keep our freedom.

We must work as hard to keep it as the colonists did
to win it.

- What might happen if Americans
  did not work to keep their freedom?

The people in Williamsburg are glad
when tourists come. Tourists spend money
in Williamsburg. They must buy food.
They must pay for places to sleep.
They may want to buy some of the things
that are sold in the shops.

- Tell how tourists and the people
  in Williamsburg depend on each other.
- What special service does Williamsburg
  provide? (Clue: How is Williamsburg
  different from most communities?)

Williamsburg was restored so that
"the future may learn from the past."

- What does this mean?
- Why is it important?

Part Three

A Great American: Thomas Jefferson

CHAPTER 1

Thomas Leaves Home

Thomas Jefferson opened his eyes early one morning. It was March, 1760. This morning he did not stay under the covers until the fireplace warmed his room. This morning was different. He jumped out of bed. Jupiter, his young servant, was just putting hot coals on the wood in the cold bedroom.

Thomas went to the washstand. He washed in the hot water that Jupiter had brought for him. Today he and Jupiter were going to start on the long road to Williamsburg.

Thomas knew that Jupiter was as excited
as he was today. He tied his red hair back
with a black ribbon. While he dressed,
Thomas talked to Jupiter. "I have heard that
there are 200 houses in Williamsburg, Jupiter."

"My, my! That's a lot of houses," said Jupiter.

"I wonder if I'll get to see the inside
of the Governor's Palace," Thomas said.

"You will be mighty busy going to school.
What is the name of that school?" Jupiter asked.

"It is the College of William and Mary,"
Thomas told him. He felt glad and proud to have
a chance to go to college. He was 17 years old.
He was old enough to go far from home.
Still, he felt a little frightened.
Would he make friends in this new town?
What would his teachers be like?

Would he miss his home here at Shadwell Plantation?
In a few days, he would find out.

It was still early morning when he and Jupiter
mounted their horses. Thomas said good-bye
to his mother and the younger children. His father
had died almost three years before. Thomas missed him.
If only his father were there waving with the others.

Many days later, Thomas and Jupiter rode
into Williamsburg. The streets were unpaved.
They were muddy from the cold spring rain.
The houses seemed so close together.

It was "public times" in Williamsburg.
"Public times" were the times when lawmakers
from all parts of Virginia came to Williamsburg.
They met at the Capitol to talk with the Governor.
Horses and carriages were everywhere.
The little shops and stores were very busy.
But Thomas saw nobody he knew. He felt so alone.
He was glad he had told Jupiter to pack his fiddle.
A fiddle was almost as good as a friend.

▶ Why was it very busy in Williamsburg
during "public times"?

In a few days, all this changed. Thomas made friends.
Most of his friends were young men at the college.
They went to dances. They went to the theater.
Sometimes there was a ball at the Raleigh Tavern.
Now the town of Williamsburg seemed happy and gay.
One of Thomas's best friends was Dr. Small.
Dr. Small was one of Thomas's teachers.
He was a fine teacher. He made it fun to learn.
Thomas wanted to read and learn more and more.
He wanted to know the answers to so many questions.
Often he would stay home from the parties.
He wanted more time to read his books.

In the summer, Thomas went for walks.
He liked to think about what he had read.
He walked down the quiet streets of Williamsburg.
The warm summer air smelled sweet with roses.
Unless it was "public times" the town seemed
sleepy and still.

Often he would walk past the Governor's Palace.
He did not think the outside of the palace was pretty.
He wondered about the inside.   Was it as beautiful
as people said?   Would he ever get to see the inside?

CHAPTER **2**

A Fiddle in the Palace

Thomas was in his second year at college when he
made two new friends. They were two of the most
important men in Williamsburg. It happened like this.
One day as Thomas finished his lessons, Dr. Small said,
"I am having dinner with some very good friends
tonight. We would like to have you come, too."

At first Thomas said, "Thank you, Dr. Small,
I should stay home and read."

But Dr. Small said, "Leave your books for one night.
I think you will find that an evening with these men
is worth many books. I have told them about you.
They would like to meet you."

The College of William and Mary—
where Thomas Jefferson went to school

"Who are these friends of yours?" Thomas asked.

"The Governor and one of Williamsburg's lawmakers, George Wythe (WYTH)," Dr. Small said.

Jupiter was even more excited than Thomas that night. "The palace! You are going to the palace with all those fine ladies and gentlemen!" Jupiter said over and over.

Thomas told him, "There will be no fine ladies this time. There will just be a few gentlemen. This is not a party or a ball."

Jupiter's eyes opened wide at this news.
"A dinner! Dr. Small must think a lot of you.
Why else would he ask you to dinner at the palace?"

"At last I'll see the inside of the palace,"
said Thomas.

The evening at the palace was wonderful.
The food was fine. Best of all, though, was the talk.
The Governor had been sent by the King
to live in Virginia. He understood the colonists
and their problems. The colonists liked him.

George Wythe knew much about laws and lawmaking.
Most people thought he was the greatest lawyer
in the colonies. He, too, understood their problems.
He also knew that good laws are very important.

Not all of the talk was about laws and taxes.
The Governor loved music. He and a few friends
played together once a week. How pleased he was
to learn that Thomas played the fiddle.
"Come and play at the palace next week," he said.

And so it happened. Thomas went to the palace
often. He listened and he learned. These three men
knew more about the colonies than could be found
in books. Each week Thomas took his fiddle
to the palace for a night of music.

- Why is it important to make good laws?
- What might be some of the colonists' problems?

In two years, Thomas finished college.
He was just 19. He wondered what he should do.
His family did not really need him at Shadwell.
His father had left him much land on the Rivanna River.
There was no house, though. The land had to be cleared
before it would be a plantation.

One day he talked to Dr. Small about his plans.
Dr. Small had an idea. "Why not learn law, Thomas?
You like reading books and learning."

"Where would I go to school?" Thomas asked.
"There are no law schools in the colonies."

"I know George Wythe would be a fine teacher,"
Dr. Small said. "He has many books, too.
Why don't we ask him to help plan your reading?"

Mr. Wythe was glad to help Thomas study law.
For five years Thomas read law books. Of course,
he went to parties and saw his young friends, too.

During those five years, England and the colonies began having trouble about taxes. The people liked their Governor. But they did not like the taxes that men in England told him to collect. Many people said there would soon be more trouble with England. Many men would be needed to help the colonists. Thomas wondered if a young lawyer could help.

- How could a man who knew about laws help the colonists?

Colonists met to talk about their problems with England. Some of the men were lawyers.

CHAPTER 3

A New Country

Thomas Jefferson soon learned that he could help.

He went to many important meetings.

Most of the meetings were held in Williamsburg.

One day Jefferson called Jupiter to him.

"We are going on a long trip," he told Jupiter.

"I must go to a meeting in Philadelphia."

It took them many days to reach Philadelphia.

Jupiter did not understand why Jefferson wanted

to go to a meeting so far from Virginia. He asked,

"Why don't they have the meeting in Williamsburg?"

Jefferson told him, "At this meeting,

there will be men from all thirteen colonies.

The King of England has been unfair.

We are having this meeting to decide what to do."

- What kind of work do you think a king does?
- Find Philadelphia on a map
  of the United States.

King George III of England

114

"Does the King know about this meeting?"
Jupiter asked.

"No, the King is far across the ocean in England,"
Jefferson said. "We have written him many letters
asking him to be fair. He has never answered
our letters. I don't think he ever will answer us.
That is why we are having this meeting."

They drove into the city of Philadelphia.
They went to the house where they were to stay.
Jupiter helped Jefferson get dressed for the meeting.
"This is almost as exciting as the first time you went
to the Governor's Palace," Jupiter said.

Jefferson was excited, too. "I wish I were better
at making speeches," he told Jupiter.
"I could be more help at the meetings.
The right thoughts and words are in my mind.
If only I could speak them the way Patrick Henry can.
What a great speaker he is!"

All of the men at the meeting soon learned
that Thomas Jefferson had many good ideas.
He did not make great speeches like Patrick Henry's.
But Jefferson could write down his thoughts very well.

At this meeting, the colonists decided
they would not obey the laws made in England.
They wanted to make their own laws.
They wanted to become a new country.
The new country would not belong to England.

They must choose someone to write their reasons
for becoming a new country. Who could write
these important words? Who could write them well?
They chose the youngest man at the meeting.
They chose Thomas Jefferson!

Jefferson worked many days at his writing.
Finally he finished. Jupiter drove him to the meeting.
Jefferson was worried. Had he written the right words?
Would the men from all the colonies like what he
had written? He climbed from the carriage.

Patrick Henry speaking at the meeting in Philadelphia

Thomas writes down reasons why the colonies
wanted to become a new country.

"I guess this is about the most important day
in my life, Jupiter," Jefferson said.

He knew that Jupiter would be waiting to hear
about the meeting. "Listen for the bell,"
Jefferson said. "If all the colonies like
what I have written, the great bell will ring."

Later that day, one of the men left the meeting.
He talked to a boy outside. The boy listened.
Then he ran up to where the bellringer waited.
Quickly he told the bellringer the news.

118